Holiday Classics

Holiday Classics

Arranged & Orchestrated by

David T. Clydesdale

Companion Materials

Choral Book	310 0519 019
Cassette	710 9891 50X
Compact Disc	710 9891 593
Cassette Trax*	310 4519 080
CD Trax**	310 9891 581
Practice Trax	310 0509 676
Studio Orchestration	310 0566 254

* The Cassette Trax provides two complete accompaniment options: Side One is in the "Split-Trax" format (left channel, instrumental; right channel, vocals minus solos) and Side Two contains stereo tracks only.

** The CD Trax is in "Split-Trax" format and provides maximum clarity and the truest music reproduction possible.

Instrumentation

Flute	Trumpet 1, 2, 3	Violin *
Oboe	French Horn 1, 2	Viola *
Clarinet	Trombone 1, 2, 3	Cello
Bass Clarinet	Tuba	Arco Bass
Alto Saxophone	Percussion	Rhythm
Tenor Saxophone		Harp
		String Reduction

* Simplified Parts Included

Edited by
Ken Barker and Rob Howard

Music Engraved by
Brent Roberts

 THIS SYMBOL INDICATES A TRACK NUMBER ON THE ACCOMPANIMENT COMPACT DISC. SELECTING A GIVEN CD TRACK NUMBER WILL START THE ACCOMPANIMENT TRACK AT THE CORRESPONDING MUSICAL SECTION INDICATED IN THE CHORAL BOOK.

DAVID T.
CLYDESDALE
MUSIC

Foreword

Most of you know that I've spent my life writing some pretty serious music. I love dramatic Easter musicals, exciting Christmas celebrations and vibrant songs of worship. This collection is totally different, and there's a reason. We have so many special guests come to our churches at Christmas, that I feel it is important to begin on common ground. By using some of the traditional favorites we all know and love, it sets the tone, relaxes everyone and lets us build from there.

I like to use these holiday classics for the first half hour, then creatively move into the deeper, true meaning of Christmas. It's been an especially effective tool of ministry for me for the past several years.

Holiday Classics is a fun, fresh approach to our traditional friends. These arrangements bring us the swing feel of "A Holly Jolly Christmas," "Winter Wonderland" and "Sleigh Ride," and the warmth of "I'll Be Home for Christmas" and "Have Yourself a Merry Little Christmas." I gave you a dance break in "The Christmas Waltz," so kick up your heels! "Grown-up Christmas List" is a bit newer, but the words are so touching and meaningful, it has already become a classic. We all know "The Twelve Days of Christmas," so a friend and I got crazy one day and created "A Dozen Daze of Christmas." It could be a classic, or it could be a big mistake—I guess you'll let me know.

This venture was a real change of pace for me, but one I thoroughly enjoyed and hope you will too. Let me be the first to wish you a very MERRY CHRISTMAS.

David T. Clydesdale

Contents

in alphabetical order

A Holly Jolly Christmas (Medley)
includes A Holly Jolly Christmas, Deck the Hall,
and Frosty, the Snow Man

Arranged by David T. Clydesdale

SMALL GROUP: Sopranos (3), Altos (3)   5   A HOLLY JOLLY CHRISTMAS (Johnny Marks)

10

11

DECK THE HALL (Traditional Welsh Carol)

ev-'ry-one you meet.

Deck the hall with boughs of hol-ly, Fa, la, la, la, la, la,

la, la, la, la. 'Tis the sea-son to be jol-ly,

Arr. © Copyright 1997 Word Music (a div. of WORD MUSIC)
All Rights Reserved.

12

14

SOLO (Tenor or low Bass singing 8vb) 45 FROSTY, THE SNOW MAN (Words & Music by Steve Nelson and Jack Rollins)

53

Fros - ty,___ the snow - man   is a fair - y tale they say,

Fros - ty,___ the snow - man,

Fros - ty,___ the snow - man,

Eb N.C.   Eb   Gm   Fm   D
                        Ab   A

he was made of snow but the chil - dren___ know   how he

unison
how he

unison
how he

unison

Eb Ebsus Eb   Fm7   D7   Cm7   Cm7
Bb   Ab   G   Ab   A   Bb

20

22

hol - ly jol - ly Christ - mas this

hol - ly jol - ly Christ - mas.

B   B/D♯   C♯   C♯/G♯   D♯m/A♯   E/G♯   F♯

91

year!

Deck the hall with boughs of hol - ly,

B   Bsus2⁴/D♯m/A♯   F♯/A♯   G♯m   F♯   B   N.C.

The Christmas Waltz

SAMMY CAHN

JULE STYNE
Arranged by David T. Clydesdale

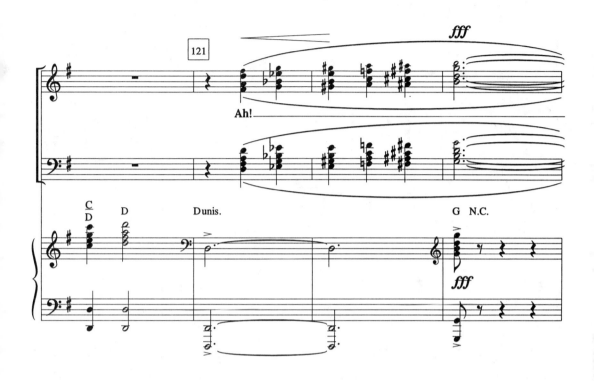

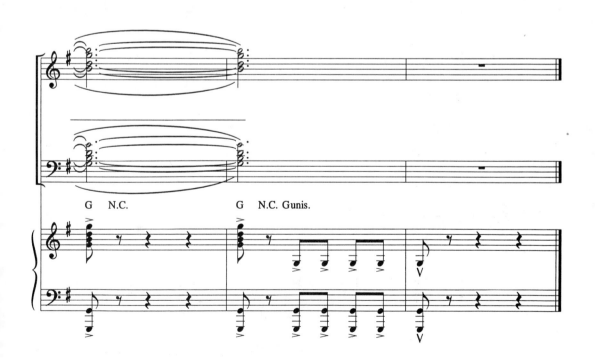

Have Yourself a Merry Little Christmas

**Words and Music by
HUGH MARTIN and RALPH BLANE**
Arranged by David T. Clydesdale

*The upper left CD points indicate the track version with trumpet solo; the lower right indicates the track version *without* trumpet solo.

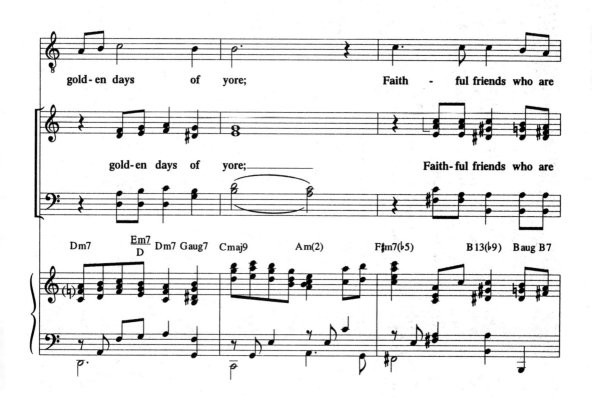

38

42

43

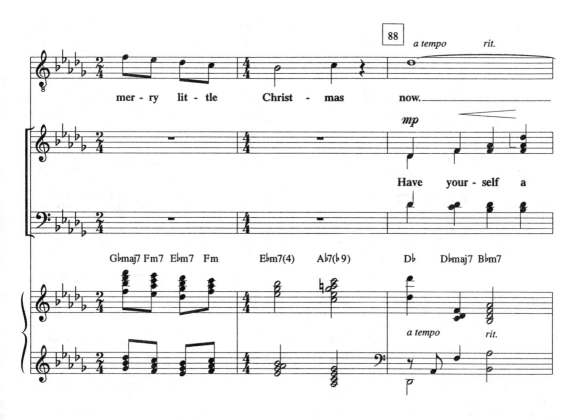

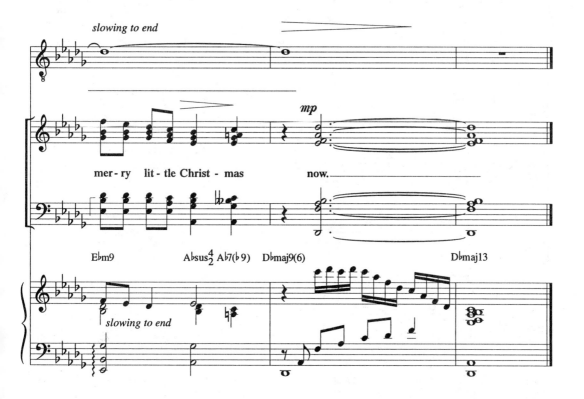

Sleigh Ride

with On a Sleigh Ride with You!

Words and Music by
DAVID T. CLYDESDALE
Arranged by David T. Clydesdale

48

21 SLEIGH RIDE (Mitchell Parish & Leroy Anderson)

come on, it's love-ly weath-er for a sleigh ride to-geth-er with

ting-gle-in', too,

C   D7   G2   Em7   Am7   D9

27

you.   Out-side the   snow is fall-ing and

with   you,   to-geth-er with you.

with   you,

G6   Em7   Am7   D   G2   Em7

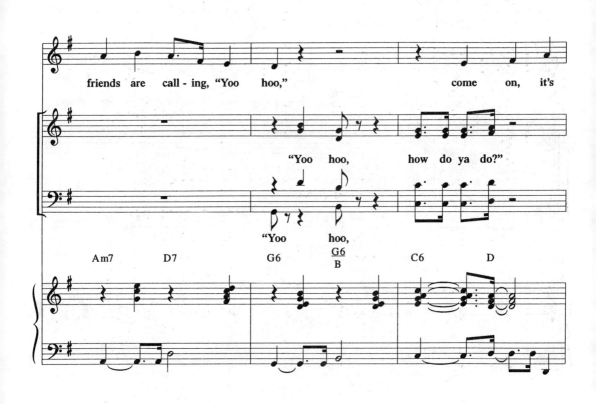

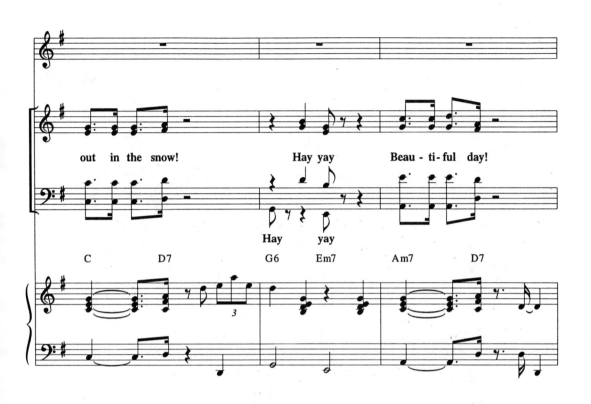

52

we've snug - gled   close to - geth - er like two   birds of a feath - er would

co - zy are we,

be.   Let's take the   road be - fore us and

tweet,   tweet,   turn up the heat!

54

58

We're glid - ing a - long with a song.——

We're glid - ing a - long of a

D9sus   N.C.   Dunis.   Dsus

75   77

Just hear those sleigh bells jin - gl-in',

win-ter-y fair - y - land.

E♭sus D♭/E♭   E♭sus   A♭2   Fm7

hoo," come on, it's love-ly weath-er for a

"Yoo hoo, how do ya do?"

"Yoo hoo,

Ab6   Ab/C   Bbm7/Db   Eb   Ab2   Fm7

sleigh ride to-geth-er with you.___

unison sub. **pp**

Let's go out in the snow!

Bbm7   Eb9sus N.C.

sub. **pp**

62

64

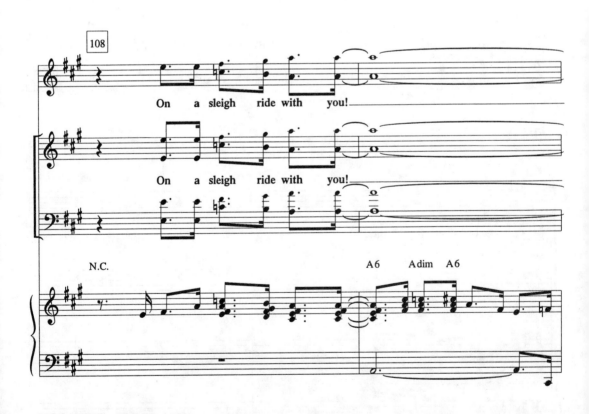

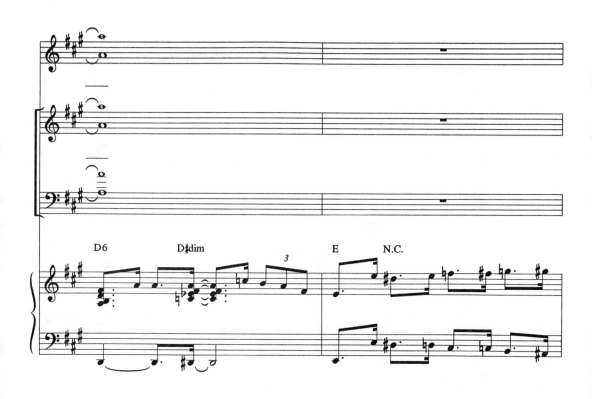

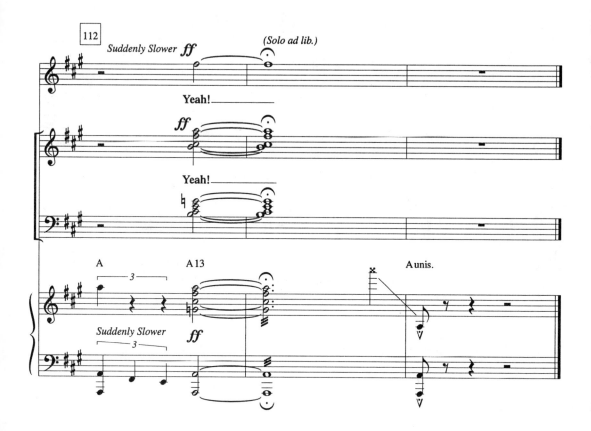

I'll Be Home for Christmas

Words and Music by
KIM GANNON and **WALTER KENT**
Arranged by David T. Clydesdale

I'm dream-ing to-night of a place I love, ev-en

more than I u-sual-ly do. And al-though I know it's a

68

70

72

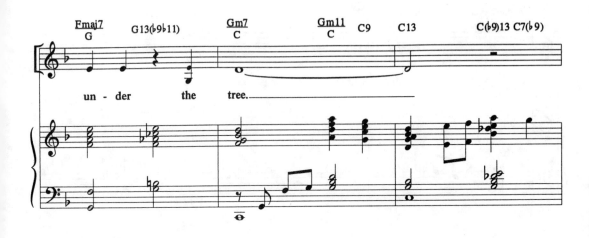

75

It's the Most Wonderful Time of the Year

Words and Music by
EDWARD POLA and **GEORGE WYLE**
Arranged by David T. Clydesdale

78

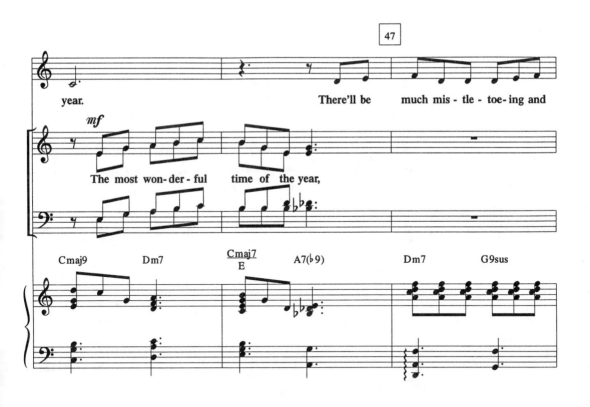

82

Christ-mas - es long, long a - go,   of Christ-mas - es   long, long a - go!   Christ-mas - es   long, long a - go!

Ebm7   Ebm7(b5)/Bb   Absus   Gb/Ab   Ebm/Gb   Fm   Ebm7   Ab

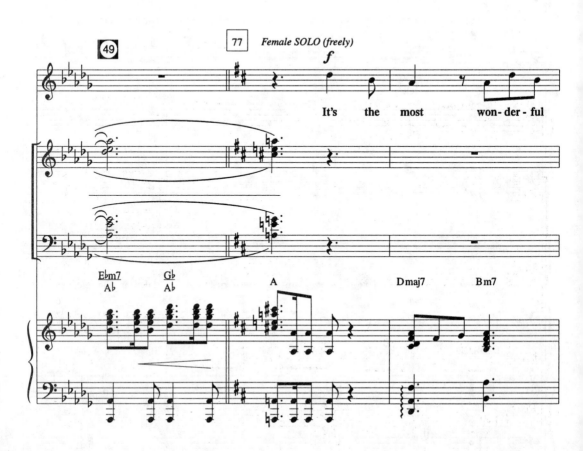

49   77   Female SOLO (freely)

It's   the   most   won-der-ful

Ebm7/Ab   Gb/Ab   A   Dmaj7   Bm7

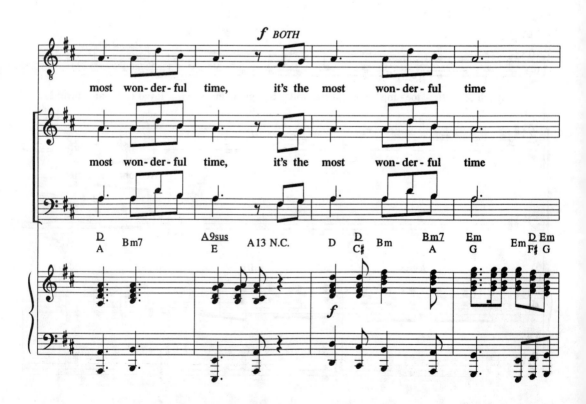

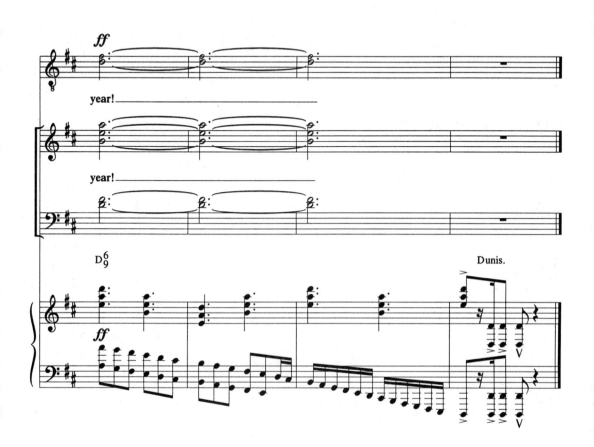

Grown-up Christmas List

Words and Music by
DAVID FOSTER and LINDA JENNER FOSTER
Arranged by David T. Clydesdale

92

friend, and right would al - ways win, and love would nev - er
have a friend, love would nev - er
D2
F♯m/B
E
C♯m7
F♯sus4/2
F♯m
25
relaxed
mp
3
end– oh, this is my grown - up Christ - mas
end– this is my grown - up Christ - mas
D♯m7(♭5)
G♯7(♭9)
G♯aug7
C♯m
F♯m7
Bm7
E7sus
relaxed

94

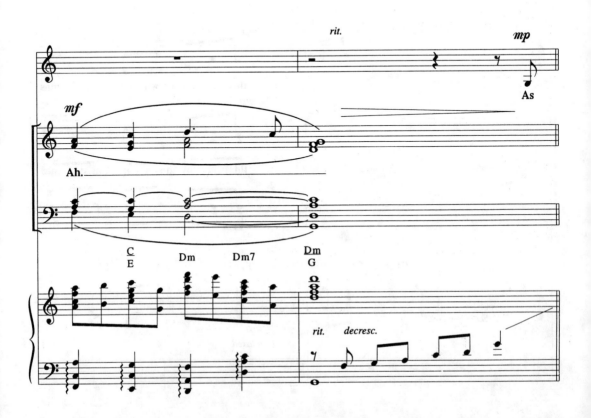

96

and time would heal___ all hearts;

start, time would heal___ all hearts;

ev - 'ry - one would have a friend,___ and right would al - ways win,

that ev - 'ry - one would have a friend,___

98

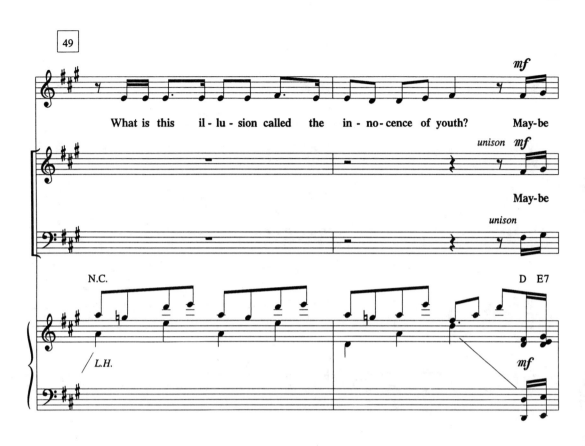

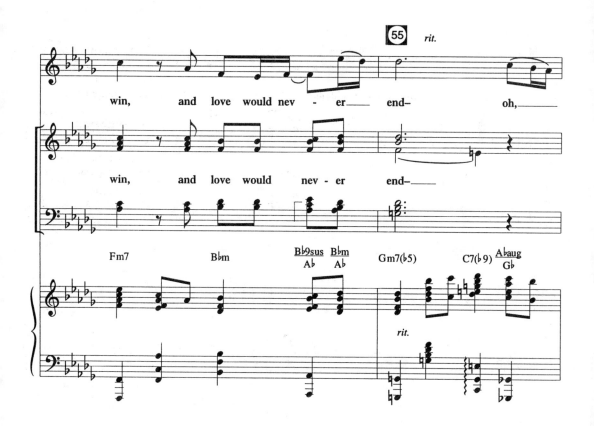

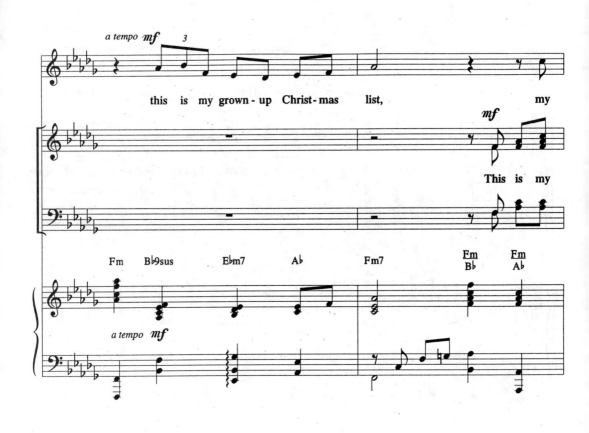

Winter Wonderland
with Let it Snow!

Arranged by David T. Clydesdale

WOMEN: *unison*

29 F#2   C#9   F#

In the mead - ow we can build a snow - man,

F#2   C#9   F#

then pre - tend that he is Par - son Brown.

He'll say, "Are you mar - ried?" We'll say, "No, man!"   But

MEN: *unison*

A2   E9   A   E/G# F#m

mf

Female SOLO (freely) 46 LET IT SNOW! (Sammy Cahn/Jule Styne)

Oh the weath-er out-side is land!

fright-ful but the fire_____ is so_____ de-

light-ful. And since we've no place to

112

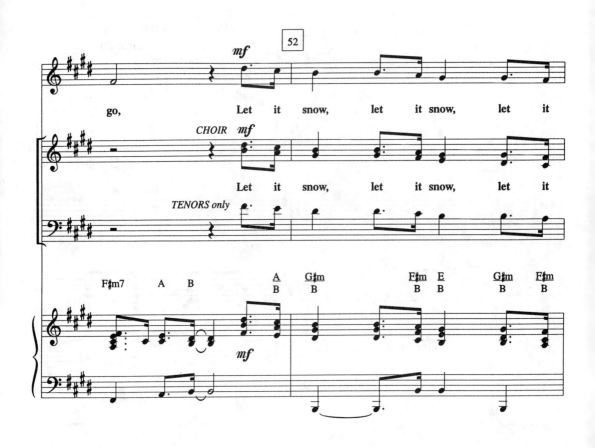

114

snow!

snow!

When we fin - al - ly kiss good - night,   how I'll

hate go - ing out in the storm!   But if you'll real - ly hold me

116

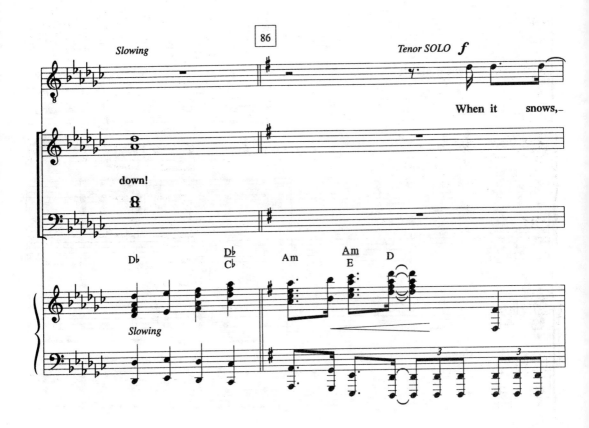

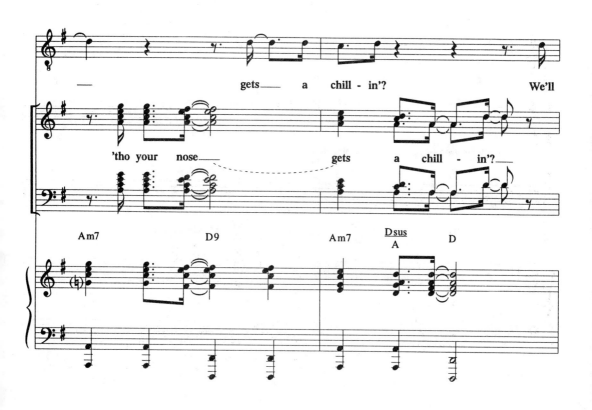

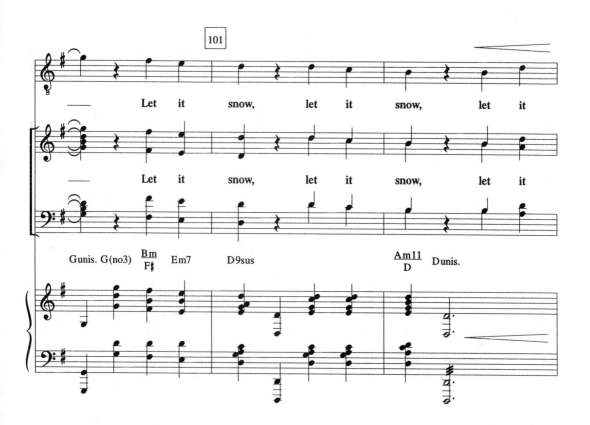

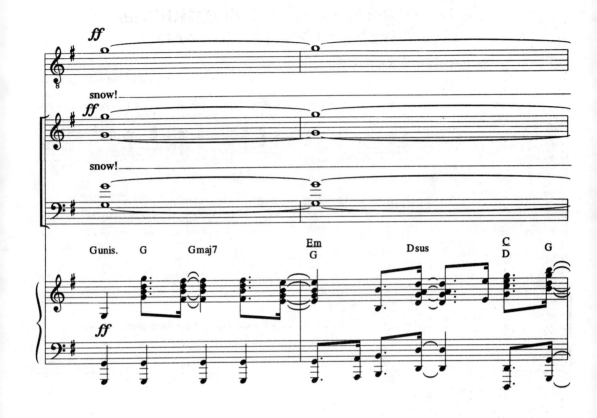

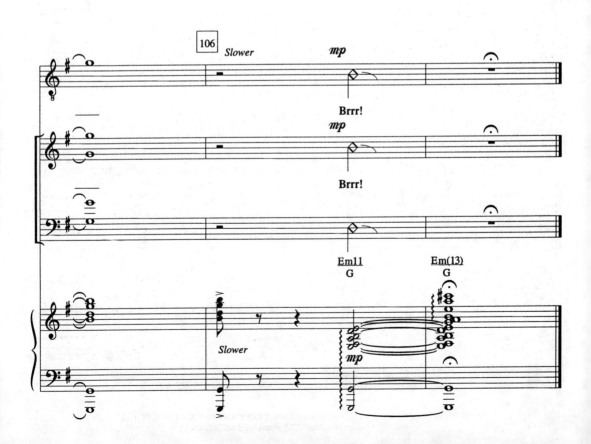

A Dozen Daze of Christmas *with*
We Wish You a Merry Christmas

DAVID A. FISCHETTE and DAVID T. CLYDESDALE

TRADITIONAL
Arranged by David T. Clydesdale

124

125

two root ca- nals   and a   Par- tridge— Fam-ily C.

D._____   5. On the   fifth   day of Christ - mas my

jewel- er gave to me: five   whole- sale   rings,_____

134

136

138

142

144 *WE WISH YOU A MERRY CHRISTMAS (Traditional British)*